TO A BRAVE MAN  'LE

WINSTON

A verse biography

Gillian Bence-Jones

TLink
2010

TLink Ltd
5 Ravenswood
Glenhurst Avenue
London NW5 1PU

First published in Great Britain by TLink Ltd 2010

Copyright© Gillian Bence Jones 2010
   All rights reserved

The moral right of the author has been asserted

This book is sold subject to the condition it shall not, by way of trade or otherwise, be lent, re-sold, hired out, or otherwise circulated without the publisher's prior consent in any form of binding or cover other than that in which it is published and without a similar condition being imposed upon the subsequent purchaser.

Printed by L&PJ Litho Ltd.

WINSTON

A verse biography

Gillian Bence-Jones

Part One
Childhood and Youth

Winston wore shorts to prep school
and was homesick. A lonely boy
in a spartan school, he missed
his reassuring nurse and he missed
his shimmering mother,
not that he saw much of her.
But a glimpse saying 'goodnight' slid him
into a sweet-smelling dream.

He wore a frogged jacket
and a shako with a plume
and rode in the charge
at Omdurman. Lickety spit
into the line of Dervishes,
while the trumpet jerked,
the hooves slammed
and the revolvers stammered.

He wore a linen suit
and got the wounded
into the train. It pulled away
and soon he was taken prisoner
by the Boers. A deeper shadow
in the shadows of the moon.
A knock and mining engineers
saw a red-haired young man.

They hid him in the mine

and presently got him away
in a railway truck.
The veering whistle on
the lonely veldt, as more than gold
moved through many miles
of dark continent
to the waves we ruled.

He wore a frock coat, bow tie,
watch chain and stood for Oldham.
Knocking on doors in streets, speaking
in half empty halls. He needed
a woman to help but his mother
wouldn't come. At last the count
in a humming hall and just,
by a few votes, he was an MP.

Some of the time, pear blossom
too early and likely to be frosted,
there was Pamela. Perhaps
she was a kingfisher, occasional,
beautiful. Pamela Plowden,
who wore a water lily
on her bottom over a silk dress
in India, causing scandal.

He earned a little money by his pen
and wrote to his mother 'I enclose
a cheque for three hundred pounds.
In a certain sense it belongs
to you, for I could never have
earned it had you not

transmitted to me the wit
and energy necessary'.

He wore a billycock hat. Hoof-beats
and ahead the wild-goose clamour of hounds.
Tied to the hounds. A hedge like
a coffin, lead-black, massive.
His horse soared. His horse adored
this crazy sport. A man was holding
the gate open. On to the road.
After the master. On! On!

Then, as now, free trade was needed;
and protection was imposed
by idiots. In this case by
Joseph Chamberlain. So Churchill
crossed the floor, left his party,
became a Liberal and was
for a long time thought of
as a turncoat, unreliable.

Part Two

Marriage

A little temple by the lake
at Blenheim. Rain on the water.
There Winston proposed to Clementine
and was accepted. The roses
took water, gave scent. 'For heaven's sake,
don't tell anybody yet'. He agreed and then
ran towards the party on the lawn
waving his arms about and shouting out
his wondrous news.

Winston wrote to her Mother
'I am not rich but Clementine
loves me and with that love I feel
strong enough to assume this sacred
responsibility. And I think I can
make her happy and give her
a career worthy of her beauty
and her many virtues'.

He wrote to Clementine
about his cousin, the Duke
of Marlborough, 'I hope you will
like my friend and fascinate
him with these strange,
mysterious eyes of yours,
whose secret I have been
trying so hard to learn.'

He delighted in their daughter
but dynasties, Field Marshals,
Dukes, buzzed in his head
when they had a son. He wrote
to his wife 'I do hope you
are being good and not sitting
up or fussing yourself. Just
get well and strong and enjoy your son'.

He became Home Secretary
and was accused ever after
of sending the troops in
to shoot the rioters and looters in
Tonypandy. He never did.
In fact, he wrote to the King 'need
for the employment of troops
is unlikely to occur'.

He spoke later about his time:
'When I was young, for two years
the light and talk faded. All was a blank.
I did my work, but it seems
to me it was the strain of crime
and punishment and all fears
of a mistaken death sentence. Dear is breath
and it is hard to leave a man to death'.

Another job. Fisher wrote
to Winston 'from the time
I knew you well I have
constantly maintained
that you were ideal for

the Admiralty because
you were a brave man'.

He changed the ships fuel
from coal to oil, although
we had no oil. He built
fifteen-inch guns, although
they were untried. He wrote
'When I saw the gun
fired and all was well
I felt I was saved from great peril.'

He wore a bathing suit
like dungarees, and played
with the children on the beach
at Cromer one Sunday in August
1914. They dammed up
little streams and Randolph
fell in, and over the placid sea
the German and British ships patrolled.

The sky fell. Germany
invaded Belgium.
What caused it?
Could it have been prevented?
Endless tears told
the helplessness of humans.
At least Winston had done
his work well; the fleet was ready.

Part Three

The Kaiser's War

At Coronel the cost
of folly was the death
of men. Churchill sent
a Capital Ship
to protect Craddock's squadron.
It was slow so it was
left behind he was out-gunned
and they all perished.

A month later the ships
that sank him steamed
into the Falklands and found
a Dreadnaught coaling there:
the tables were turned. Craddock
was revenged. After
four months of war the sea
was clear of German ships.

Antwerp was besieged and Winston managed
to get himself sent there. Before long
he wanted to resign from the Admiralty
and take charge. The Cabinet laughed
and refused. As he was coming home,
his wife had a red-haired daughter
whom they called Sarah. Lively
beautiful and wilful from the first.

In 1915 he formed

'The Landships Committee'
of the Admiralty
under the presidency of
Mr Tennyson-d'Eyncourt
and the chain of action
led to the first use of tanks
in August 1916.

The Navy tried to go through
the Dardanelles and lost
three ships to mines. The ships
were old. The loss of life
was slight but the Admiral
in charge lost his nerve.
So did Fisher, and Churchill
couldn't persuade them to try again.

Instead they invaded Gallipoli,
didn't press it home.
and got stuck there. The Cabinet
tottered. Fisher disappeared.
The Prime Minister decided
to form a coalition
with the Conservatives
and Winston lost his job.

About then one week-end
he found his sister-in-law painting
in the garden and said 'That looks
rather fun. Can I have a go?'
He tried, didn't like water-colour,
couldn't mix oils, so rang up

14

Sir John Lavery, who came
and was helpful and encouraging.

He wore khaki and served
with the Grenadiers.
My father-in-law met him
in the trenches and said,
'You've got the wrong helmet.'
He was annoyed and said
he'd been told it was
much the best sort.

'Far from it. I'll show you.
Give it here!' my father-in-law
said. He took the helmet, threw
it high and then put
two bullets in it
before it landed. They both
went right through. 'Heavens!' said
Churchill, 'You're right. It's no good.'

He was soon commanding
a battalion but it was disbanded
for lack of men and he returned.
Asquith was out-manoeuvered by
Lloyd- George who then became
Prime Minister. He wanted Winston
in his Government but Northcliffe
and the Tories didn't.

Churchill wrote of this time 'Surely
to no nation had fate been

more malignant than to Russia'.
Her ship went down in sight of port.
The long retreats were ended, arms
were pouring in. They only needed
to endure to enjoy the fruits
of general victory.

'We may measure the strength of Russia
by the battering it had sustained,
by the disasters it had endured
and by the recovery it had made.
Nicholas II was only a true,
simple man of average ability.
He was struck down and delivered
with all he loved to death'.

Winston wore a top hat
and was made Minister
for Munitions. In 1917
in November his beloved tanks
went into action at Cambrai.
They swept all before them,
but, as few had expected it,
there were no reserves.

In March 1918
Churchill was at the Armoury
in Montreuil to settle the tank program.
After lunch Sir Douglas Haig
explained the situation. He was
daily expecting an attack. Winston
visited General Tudor who

was a friend since India.

He wrote 'We received a hearty welcome
when we arrived after dark
upon a tranquil front. The next day
a deathly silence brooded over
the front. Yet the sunlit fields
were instinct with foreboding. I woke
that night at four and lay musing.
Suddenly the silence was broken.

'And then there rose the most tremendous
cannonade I shall ever hear.
I dressed and went out. On the duckboards
I met Tudor. "This is it,"
he said. The front swept around us
in a wide curve of leaping flame.
There arose continuously the larger flames
of exploding magazines.
'It was my duty to leave the scene
and with mingled emotions
I bade my friends farewell. Tudor
seemed an iron peg hammered
into icy ground. And so it proved.
It was the greatest onslaught in the history
of the world, and the Germans had
a superiority of four to one.

'Backward across the hideous desolation
of the old crater fields rolled
the British front for five days.
But the Germans losses were much

greater than the British losses.
Irreparable, sounding the knell of doom,
and they did not drive us to the coast,
or part the French and English'.

Thanks to Winston and his workers,
who gave up their holidays,
the weapons were soon replaced.
The Americans were pouring in,
young, tall and not tired.
'All felt,' wrote a Frenchman, 'life
arriving in floods to reanimate
France, bled white by war.'

Winston's arrangements with
the Americans worked excellently
and he became 'the Nitrate King.'
In July 1918 the Germans
drove for Paris, but the French
attacked the drive with light tanks
and broke through. On August 8th
in the half light of a misty dawn

The British tanks rolled forward
into No-Man's-Land. Two British,
four Canadian and four tough
Australian divisions
followed and victory was complete.
In two hours the British took
sixteen thousand prisoners
and two hundred guns.

Winston wrote 'I spent two days
on the battlefield. When news
of a great tank victory
began to come through I got
into my aeroplane and took
a couple of days holiday.
Rawlinson was at Amiens.

'I was delayed getting there
by columns of German prisoners
which endlessly streamed along the dusty roads.
No one who has been a prisoner of war
himself can be indifferent to the lot
of prisoners. The sad
expression of the officers contrasted
sharply with the cheerful soldiers.

'General Rawlinson received me
with his customary good humour
and at lunch explained his victory.
Using new weapons as they should
be used, he had reaped swift reward.
I had known him since Omdurman
where he was one of Kitchener's
leading Staff Officers.

'The battle was still in full blast
and I asked how best to see it.
"There's a road from Amiens to Vermont
It's being shelled but it's clear. Go ahead."
So off we went through ghostly Amiens.
The German dead lay everywhere.

Cavalry cantered gaily about.
A solider said, "Best we've ever had."

In September an Australian
division captured Mont St Quentin
and the Allies advanced. Foch wrote
'The operations of the British Army
in August would serve as a model for all time.'
Meanwhile Clementine, much concerned
with her canteens, was having
another baby.

In late September at great cost
the allies broke the Hindenberg line.
In October Germany
sued for peace. There was a delay
while men died and Wilson proposed
his fourteen points. But in November
it was all over. France was free
and determined to be revenged.

It was all over. But is it
ever over? My father's cousin
was killed in the turret of *The Lion* at Jutland
and that was the end of an old family.
My Governess told me once
'There was a boy, but he was killed
in France.' One of our men had been
gassed and often fought for breath.

Winston knew. Which was why
he favoured tanks and the Dardanelles.

He wrote 'All the great offensives
were failures. The Generals
opposed a hail of bullets
with the breasts of gallant men
under the fatal illusion
that this was waging war'.

Part Four

Between the Wars

Soon after the war was over
they had another child,
another red-haired daughter,
and Winston was beguiled.
Just as the troops came home again,
just as the days grew cold,
just as people breathed again,
they called her Marigold.

Winston was Secretary of State
for war. He wanted to learn
to fly. One day the controls failed
as they began to turn
above Croydon. Winston was bruised
but spoke at a dinner given that night
for General Pershing.

Weakened as they were by the war,
they had little strength for the flu,
which killed more than the war.
The epidemic grew
and Isabelle, the Churchills' Nanny,
got it, and, being off her head,
delirious with the disease, took
the baby to her bed.

There was no hope of a doctor till day.
Clementine took away

the screaming baby and went up and down
between where the girl lay
and where the child yelled. All night
she and a housemaid tried
to keep the girl's temperature down
but as day dawned she died.

Then they had an anxious wait
to see if the small baby
got the disease, which would most likely
be fatal, but luckily
she didn't. Winston's mother
wore high-heeled shoes
and fell. Her broken leg went wrong.
When Winston heard the news

That she was dying, he ran through the streets.
But for all his pains
he was too late. He wrote 'The wine
of life was in her veins.
Sorrows and storms were conquered by her nature.
She didn't care to repine.
I feel loss, but on the whole
it was a life of sunshine.'

Winston became Colonial Secretary
and took Clementine
to Cairo. They went to see the Pyramids
in the snug sunshine
with Lawrence of Arabia, who told them
the villagers still hailed
their Pharaohs. If a mummy passed

they came down and wailed.

Then to Jerusalem where
Winston carried out
a British policy, favoured
by Americans, about
a Palestinian homeland for
the Jews. The two sides
seemed irreconcilable.
He worried, but let it slide.

Marigold, a lovely child,
they called 'Duckadilly',
Diana, 'the gold-cream kitten',
Sarah, 'Bumblebee',
and Randolph, 'the rabbit'. Marigold
sang rather well
'I'm forever blowing bubbles'.
Clean and tinkling as a bell.

In July the children went to Broadstairs
and soon Randolph wrote
'On Sunday we went out to sea
in a little rowing boat.
Marigold's been rather ill
but is now much better'
'Baba is quite well again,'
said Sarah's letter.

But it did not last. Soon her throat
was very sore again.
It turned to septicemia.

The doctor fought in vain.
Her parents were sent for and as
her mother sat by her bed
one evening in late August
she suddenly said,

'Sing me bubble!'. Her mother,
struggling with tiredness and sorrow,
began the plaintive song.
'Not tonight - finish tomorrow!'
whispered the child. She died next day.
Like an animal in pain,
Clementine shrieked. They buried the child
in London in the rain.

They went to Scotland. Winston stayed
longer painting and wrote sadly
'Alas I keep on feeling the hurt
of the Duckadilly.'
In 1932 Winston
bought Chartwell, where
he was happy. But Clementine
knew it was too dear.

In the same year they had
another child, Mary,
and the Government fell
very suddenly.
At the election the Liberals
had a great defeat
and, like many Liberals,
Winston lost his seat.

In 1924 the Tories
came back to free trade.
So Winston came back to the Tories
and went, where he stayed
for forty years, to Essex. Soon
adopted, then elected,
he was made Chancellor,
with Baldwin at the head.

About this time he went to Rome
and was asked to meet the Pope.
They were polite but of real contact
there seemed but little hope.
'Daddy hates the Communists,'
the child Randolph said.
'You feel they are a danger?'
asked the Pope, nodding his head.

'The greatest danger this suffering world
has had to endure,'
After that the Pope and Winston were
always apt to assure
everyone the other was
a well informed man.
In '26 there was a strike
in which Winston ran

The British Gazette, with a
circulation of about three million.
In '29 Winston lost his post
to an election and planned
to go to America. His wife

had been ill and could
not go. The Americans were gambling.
Winston understood

The Stock Exchange was going up,
so he gambled, too.
After the crash in October
he soon came to rue
his recklessness. I read
in an autobiography
by a keeper how Winston
came to shoot in January

And the keeper was told to find
a quiet donkey so
Mr. Churchill could ride between drives.
'His ankle's bad you know,
he broke it in America.'
All went merrily
till the last drive when Winston
shot sitting on the donkey

Which took some restraining. The keeper
wished he'd only brought
his camera. William Nicholson
painted a scene which caught
Winston and Clementine at Chartwell.
Always afterwards Churchill
said 'in painting he was the person
who taught me most.'

The games people play, including

love, are seldom framed
better than in a country house.
At Chartwell they talked and gamed,
and worked and walked about,
and there, when the weather was fine,
Churchill painted and Charlie Chaplin
sat outside with Albert Einstein.

In 1935 Hitler
announced his Air Force
was as large as the British Force.
Winston wrote 'This, of course,
makes Baldwin's statements
completely false
and justifies the assertions
that I have made'.

Winston would gamble. Clementine
hated it. One late night
she left him in the Casino.
She woke at first light.
Something rustled. Winston had
completely covered her bed
with notes. He'd won for once
and painted the bed red.

Later when she was abroad
Winston wrote to his wife
'Far and away the most precious
thing I have in life
Is your love for me'. They differed,
though, over the Abdication.

He hoped a way could be found;
she agreed with most of the nation.

The King appealed to Winston who felt
great loyalty.
He spoke in the Commons but
not successfully.
After Baldwin's statement Winston
rose and asked that no
irrevocable step should be taken.
Cries of 'Sit down!' and 'Oh!'

And 'No!' from all sides. Later, when
King George was crowned and his Queen
made her vows, Winston whispered
to his wife, 'You've been
right all along. I see now
the other wouldn't have done.'
Soon after the Coronation in
'37 the danger began:

Spain, the Nazis grabbing Austria.
Churchill's star was low
and he was depressed. People said
it all went to show
what a wrong-minded man
he was. War-monger, too.
The BBC wouldn't let him broadcast.
He hadn't enough to do.

He cheered himself up slightly
and the House greatly

when Nancy Astor told him during
an argument 'Really,
If you were my husband I think
after a little bit
I'd poison your tea.' 'If you were my wife,'
said Winston, 'I'd drink it.'

In 1937
the next thing
after Hitler invaded
was Munich. The din
of great rejoicing drowned Winston's
lament for our betrayal
of Czechoslovakia. Most people
knew the peace was frail.

In August 1939
Russia and Germany
signed a pact. Russia gave Hitler
oil and all was harmony
as they decided to divide Poland.
I remember hearing
Chamberlain's speech as I played
and somehow fearing

that man was sad. 'Someone ought
to give him a sweet,'
I thought. Then all the grownups,
in spite of the lovely heat,
seemed sad too and told me
we were at war.
I didn't know what that meant,
having seldom heard of it before.

Part Five

Hitler's War

Chamberlain made Churchill first Lord.
It was like old times and all
that Admiralty House could afford
was theirs. Winston wrote of this recall
'So it was that I was escorted
to the room I had before my fall'.
To the fleet, waiting for an attack
the signal went out 'Winston is back'.

The phony war had us in its clutches.
Nothing happened endlessly
by land, but a great deal too much
and too tragic happened at sea.
Rations, gas masks, shortages, such
was our life. Pamela Digby
married Randolph, who was filled
with zeal to have sons before he was killed.

Clementine in early spring
launched the carrier *Indomitable*
and Winston painted, pretty thing,
a picture of her doing it. Unable
to stop the Germans swallowing
Norway, because of air power, our forces
withdrew, defeated by the stars in their courses.

The Prime Minister asked Labour
to join in a National Government.

They only would under a new leader
and so before long the King sent
for Winston, who wrote of this later
'I felt all my past life had been spent
preparing. All my testimony
was now. I was walking with destiny'.

He soon spoke in the House. 'As yet
I have nothing to offer but
blood, toil, tears and sweat'.
As he spoke the Germans shut
the door on the phony war and let
their panzer hounds tear the guts
out of France,. On the phone their heated
Prime Minister said 'We have been defeated'.

Winston went to France, continually
advising, encouraging.
The German troops eventually
reached the coast of France, cutting
off the British Forces. Then we heard
the word where meaning
and feeling and memory lurk
for so many people: Dunkirk.

The little ships went out in the heat,
waited under the shells to fill
and go back to England to repeat
the whole process. Even now we still
remember Winston's speech:
'We shall fight on the beaches,
We shall fight in the streets,

We shall fight on the hills,
We shall never surrender',
giving comfort to the defenders.

In June 1940 Italy
declared war on us. France
fell. De Gaulle flew boldly
to Britain and set up 'le Resistance.'
Winston's youngest daughter, Mary,
wrote later of ambience
and 'how these days seemed to chill and seethe.
Never again could one scarcely breathe'.

The blitz began and one night
the Churchills were dining with colleagues when
Winston went at the noisy height
of a raid and told the cook and kitchen-
maid and servants to shelter. A slight
argument ensued, but then
they went and soon the kitchen windows broke,
filling it with glass, plaster and smoke.

Winston wore a bath towel and went
dripping across the road to
the flat in St James, where they spent
the rest of the war. One night he knew
most of the Docks and City burnt
in one huge bonfire
from one of his many calls,
and growled out 'Save St. Paul's!'

Many of the Londoners wrote

to Clementine. They would speak
of shelters, some leaked and, (I quote)
'Bedding should be stored twice a week
or lice must spread'. They also note
bunks were too small. She went to seek
the facts in a shelter and spoke in one
and then Winston got something done.

That December the Eighth Army
drove the Italians out of Egypt
and Churchill and his family
christened little Winston and sipped
a toast to Christ's new solider. Happy
at Christmas, they all slipped
into forgetting the war
and celebrated as they often had before.

In 1941 the Yanks
gave us ships and tanks and guns
with Lend Lease. Rommel and his tanks
of the Afrika Korps won
back most of Egypt and thanks
to Hitler we had the Russians
to help. Winston said 'If Hitler invades hell
I shall form an alliance with the devil'.

But while Hitler invaded Russia
the Churchills travelled to bombed cities
in a special train. As far
as Clyde and Hull. But the scars
of war were the same. The bravery,
the ruins, the houses open to the sky

often made the Churchills cry.

Over the rubble people came running.
In refugee shelters they clapped and cheered.
Clementine wore turbans. Her style was stunning,
and all the while she helped and steered
the 'Aid to Russia Fund'. The cunning
Roosevelt saw Winston and cleared
up many things in Newfoundland;
a first meeting for these renowned hands.

Winston wore a siren suit -
'Rompers' his family called it -
and worked at night, alert, astute,
and suddenly funny. He stayed fit
and indefatigable . The long route
to victory opened up but
it involved a far war
when the Japs bombed Pearl Harbour.

At Christmas 1942
he went over to Washington
and , although nobody knew,
had a slight heart attack. He'd gone
to speak to Congress and all through
those desperate days we managed to cling on
to Malta, which was, as once before,
the gold key to the world's door.

The Repulse and *The Prince of Wales*
were sent out to Singapore.
Rumors ran wild, intelligence failed.

The Japanese planes were more
far reaching than we knew. They nailed
the two big ships with bombs before
our planes arrived. After that we found
the Pacific was a Japanese playground.

They took Hong Kong, they landed in Malaya,
while Churchill went to Washington
and spent Christmas there, far
from home, and gave a speech on
the war to Congress. In Libya,
the snows of Russia and Malaya,
in the jungle and on the seas beside
hosts of men fought and died.

Singapore fell. Doom fell
on the East and sadly a thousand men
were forced to live and work in the hell
of a Japanese camp. And when
some of them were freed, the spell
of white prestige and power was broken.
For the prisoners hunger and pain.
Some were never healthy again.

Randolph and Pam fell out.
Soon she loved Averil Harriman.
Randolph made many scenes about
his wrongs. His parents wouldn't understand
how much more serious his complaints
were than the war. So then to show
Pam he became a commando.

In October they fought in the heat
for twelve days at Alamein.
The allies won. Winston would repeat
'Before Alamein no victories, but again
after Alamein we never had defeat.'
He insisted on having the refrain.
For the first time for years, the swell
and glorious tumble of the bells.

In early '43 Winston went
to Casablanca and then on to Turkey.
He met Roosevelt and spent
a few hours painting. But the
planes were cramped and inclement.
He got pneumonia and all February
he was pretty ill. In May one war ceased:
the Germans surrendered in the Middle East.

In summer Clementine and Winston
with their daughters Sarah and Mary
went on the 13th of June
to the Guildhall to be made freemen
of the shattered city of London.
Mary wrote much later 'We
drove with them in the open landau
for the highest honors London can bestow.'

In July the allies landed in Sicily
Admiral Cunningham
signaled to the Admiralty
'Weather not favourable but am
proceeding'. Some Italians wanted to scram

and come to surrender. While they collided
with each other, the Germans decided.

In August Winston was off again.
Quebec, Washington, then
in November to Teheran
to meet Roosevelt and Stalin.
Roosevelt knew Stalin was a man
of the people. The rich were vain.
His meetings with Winston were deferred.
Communism was much preferred.

Winston wanted to talk to the generals
and so flew to Eisenhower's place
near Carthage, where his travels
caught up with him. By the grace
of God he'd brought his doctor. His trials
were long, pneumonia again. The case
was serious and so about
Christmas time Clemmie flew out.

As long as Winston rested he felt fine.
So while he had to do this,
Sarah, then Clementine.
read him Pride and Prejudice.
With lots of good food and wine,
they didn't really seem to miss
Christmas at home. A tin-roofed
hut was their church, as Winston improved.

The date arrived but the weather was bad.
Postponed for a day: Winston thrilled,

wanted to go, too, and had
to be restrained by the King. Filled
with pride, in the map room, he said
'Twenty thousand men may be killed
before morning'. News came; they were in,
with a long way to go before Berlin.

'We fought them on the beaches'
but they weren't our beaches. Sword,
Juno, Gold. History teaches
the details on the beaches and abroad,
where each regiment reaches
each day, the defence, the record.
And where they fought and died that day
on the long beaches children play.

Four days later Winston went
to France in a destroyer and found
General Montgomery in a tent.
To battle sounds
they lunched by the lake and spent
a few hours on the German ground.
Returning, they passed our ships firing at the Hun
and Winston got the Admiral to fire his guns.

Only a few days after this
the first flying bomb appeared.
Hard on a tired people. You couldn't miss
that noise. You always feared
it would stop. I remember this
and seeing three of those weird
birds the night one smashed the spire,

lighting up the land with dragon fire.

Ivan Cobbold was reading
the lesson in the Guards Chapel,
none of the congregation heeding.
Doodlebugs endless rumble.
One cut out. Ivan went on reading.
After a few seconds of rustling glide
one hundred and thirty-one people died.

Winston wrote of these happenings:
'Dawn brought no relief and cloud
no comfort. Going home in the evenings
a man never knew what he'd find. Cowed
by sleeplessness, his wife could cling
to no surety of his return.' The bombs
growled over. Eight thousand were launched
against London and six thousand people were killed.

Winston saw Parliament retire
to the steel Church House and there
one of the MP's inquired
'Why are we back in here?'
Another MP at once fired
'Go and look in Birdcage Walk where
you'll see the answer'. A vile, tense,
universal, long silence.

In July Winston was back in France.
He saw landing craft bringing
tanks and watched the allied advance
from a Storch plane. The singing

in the mess gave him the chance
to teach the officers the ringing
words of 'Rule Britannia', which chanced
to rather fit the circumstances:

'The nations not so blessed as thee
shall in their turn to tyrants fall
whilst thou shalt flourish,
Shalt flourish proud and free,
the dread and envy of them all.'

In July the German Generals tried
to kill Hitler but somehow
a strong table saved him. He cried
out 'Who will believe now
that God does not preserve me?' Four died.
The answer to his question, 'Somehow,'
the British said with a groan,
'the devil looks after his own.'

In August Winston flew to Italy
and watched the Americans invade
the South of France, which he
had tried to prevent, planning a raid
to get to Vienna and then maybe
Poland before the Russians. He stayed
in Alexander's Palace near Sienna,
fretting about the drive to Vienna.

Soon the Russians got very near
to Warsaw and called on all
the inhabitants to rise. It's clear

they meant to cut as many of the tall
Polish poppies as they could. From near
they never got nearer, while the walls
of Warsaw fell. There was no water
and the Nazis completed the slaughter.

The Russians wouldn't let us use
their airports to get supplies
and weapons to Warsaw . As the news
reached the cabinet, it 'gave rise
to deep anger', Winston wrote. His news
grew stronger as the frantic cries
for help swelled. The last broadcast they could give
said 'Poland lives while the Poles live.'

In late August Paris fell
to Leclerc who wrote to de Gaulle
'I have an impression this is still
1940 before the long haul,
but the other way on. They, as well
as us then, seem off the ball,
disorganized'. Hitler, evilly discerning
as ever, asked 'Is Paris burning?'

In September just then
the first rocket arrived.
They killed twice as many when
they hit, as flying bombs continued
to do. No warning, no defence. Our men
and airmen overran and dived
the launching sites. But for half a year
the Londoners live with still more fear.

In September Winston went
to Canada again and then
Washington. The armies spent
a lot of time fighting and when
they got to Germany it meant
worse fighting. The navies, swollen
with new ships, fought in the China sea
and the Divine wind blew ferociously.

In October he was off again
to Moscow where Stalin welcomed him
and introduced him to the Quisling pains
who were to govern Poland. They were grim
and no one took to them, though the main
detractors were the Poles whose slim
authority was ebbing. The Government in London
hoped to be the rulers with the Huns gone.

In December Rundstedt attacked
in the Ardennes and broke the line.
The weather was bad so the allies lacked
air power. Although it was a sign
they weren't finished yet, the packed
German tanks lost many men.
They thought the Yanks wouldn't fight
but soon found they fought all right.

After the Germans left Greece
the communists took over. Winston
sent some British troops. No peace
and the Greek king, who would have gone,

felt he had no right till Greece
had held a plebiscite on
Monarchy. They were fighting so
Winston knew that he must go.

He knew it on Christmas Eve. His wife,
who'd worked so hard and had half the family
staying, cried. He had the time of his life
in Athens under fire and comfortably
in the destroyer *Ajax*. Fighting was rife.
The communists held half the city.
Finding the Archbishop diligent,
Winston got the king to make him Regent.

In January '45
he was off again. This time
to Yalta. To talk and eat and strive
with Stalin over the coming crime
of stealing Poland. The stinging hive
of Europe stirred. The long time
of Roosevelt was growing very short
but he could handle Stalin, as he thought.

The General in charge in Greece, Scobie,
decided the communists would attack
at Christmas. So the infantry
was kept on alert. The whole pack
besieged them very early
on Boxing Day. They fought back.
When all was quiet again a belated
'Scobiemas' was celebrated.

'I deserved to see the crossing
of the Rhine' wrote Winston,
so off he flew, enjoying
the danger. Monty took him on
a launch over the river, strolling
on the German side, then upon
a high broken bridge till the descent
of shells close-by showed it was time they went.

In March the communists began to ignore
the agreements in Romania
and Poland. Winston wrote 'as before
I telegraphed to Roosevelt. I fear
he wasn't listening anymore.'
And so for thirty years
ten pleasant nations fell
into a sort of living hell.

Winston wrote later 'this was to me
a most unhappy time. I sat
at table with blessings from every
part of the Alliance at
Parliament with painfully
aching heart and a feeling that
was forbidding, hardly proud,
although I moved through cheering crowds'.

Roosevelt died in April
suddenly. Parliament
was closed for him. 'We will
miss his leadership. He lent
us ships with Lend Lease' Churchill

said'. It was soon evident
Roosevelt , with his arrogant touch,
had not told Truman much.

Hitler killed himself. In May
the war was over. A haul
to get the men home. They
sent the anti-Nazis from all
the prisons first. One fine day
the King and Queen went to St. Paul's
with the Churchills and all races and ranks
after the dangerous years to give thanks.

Part Six

After the War

My Mother took me all the way
to London for VE day.
I found it noisy and stony
but I was glad I'd been
because we saw the King and Queen
on the palace balcony.

All the people in the street
and the ones we chanced to meet
were happy and friendly, excited.
It seemed special, dazing,
as if we'd done something amazing.
Giants slain, wrongs righted.

Liberals and Labour wouldn't
serve any longer, couldn't
wait till the end of the war,
so the whole battered collection
had a khaki election.
I never remembered one before.

Most people thought they knew
the Tories would win. Churchill, too,
thought that, then woke with a sob
and knew it was bad. Many lines
of posters of him with the V sign
and 'Help him finish the job.'

Clementine, opening her eyes,
said 'Perhaps a blessing in disguise.'
Winston, somewhat surprised,
replied with ready wit,
'Seems to me it's
remarkably well disguised.'

There was nothing then.
No red boxes when
he was out: fired.
No plans for calls, or cares.
He had to be carried upstairs.
He was so very tired.

The Americans dropped
two atom bombs. The war stopped.
Six weeks before the war's cease,
before Hiroshima, before
Nagasaki. Six weeks and more.
Japan sued for peace.

Winston went to Italy
where he painted peacefully
and wrote in a warm letter
to his wife. 'It has done me
no end of good.' He knew he
was slowly getting better.

The Churchills went where the sun shone
in America that winter. Winston
made a speech about the Iron Curtain,
which annoyed people. They

were hopeful and innocent as May;
he was better informed and certain.

I remember that time well.
We were mostly hungry as hell,
and cold too. The Labour party
cut the rations. They rationed bread.
We had powdered eggs instead
of real ones. They still rationed tea.

Churchill said in the House 'I wish
that in an island surrounded by fish
and made largely of coal those oddities
over the way did not stage
a prolonged and acute shortage
of both those commodities'.

The hardships and shortages we carried
grew lighter when the Princess got married.
Winston and Clementine, too,
were invited to attend.
Clemmie wrote to an old friend
'It really seems too good to be true'.

In summer 1949,
in Italy, without any sign
of warning, Winston had a stroke.
They decided not to tell,
especially as he soon got well.
They said it was a chill from a soak.

In '50 there was an election.

Labour again by a tiny fraction.
We were all tired and cowed.
Houses short. You'd little chance
of travel with that allowance.
Everything was 'not allowed'.

Their friends put money in a trust for them
and with that endowment they worked to stem
the expenses at Chartwell by giving it
to the National Trust. Mary
married Soames, who subsequently
ran Chartwell to its profit.

Soames took Winston racing. Of course,
he loved it and bought a horse.
Clementine was somewhat riled
but the horse won many a race.
She saw the smile on Winston's face
and became reconciled.

In '52 the Government fell.
We felt we'd come out of the spell
of bitter winter. We trusted Winston
to bring back prosperity
after the long hardships going on and on
and the endless austerity.

The King asked Winston to form a government
and he did so immediately, which meant
their moving back to Number Ten.
He was seventy six but fit
except for deafness and a bit

of confused speech now and then.

'52. In February
the Princess was high up in a tree
in Kenya, watching elephants in a deep
water hole. Moonlight quivered on the trunk,
antelope came down to drink
and the King died in his sleep.

Winston was sad. They'd fought a war
together and he admired the poor
hard pressed King. But all his keen
instincts of burning loyalty
and ever-present chivalry
found their ideal in the young Queen.

As William Cecil's experience bought
influence for the Queen and Melbourne taught
Victoria, so Winston gave
his knowledge to Elizabeth,
glad to find, before his death,
affinity, both of them dutiful and brave.

He accepted from the Queen that thing
he'd refused eight years before from the King:
the Garter. A letter came designed
to please. 'I am not able to say
what we all feel, so send today
the best halibut I could find.'

At the coronation Churchill
for once had more than his fill

of ceremony in the front of the Abbey.
Riding in a coach in the rain
with an escort was a strain,
but he enjoyed it tremendously.

The Prime Minister of Italy
was given a banquet. Suddenly
Winston's son-in-law, Soames
noticed Winston couldn't rise.
He'd had another stroke. Surprise
didn't stop them smuggling him home.

Doctors came in the morning.
Winston insisted on attending
a cabinet meeting. Only one man
noticed. He rang up, which meant,
as Mary asked, he was silent.
His name was Harold Macmillan.

The doctors proclaimed Winston must rest.
They went to Chartwell, which was best
for privacy. Staying there for a bit,
he slowly but surely got well
and no one, no press, could tell.
They'd somehow got away with it.

Of course it was very wrong
but Winston's zest for life was strong
and he felt sure only he
could deal with Russia and its head,
Kruschev, now Stalin was dead.
Just a little longer maybe.

Next year, in '54, Winston
was eighty. His happiness shone
at the Palace and in the House
where they gave a party for him
and a picture by Sutherland
that he didn't understand
and so began to curse and grouse.

He had liked Sutherland so much
during the sittings. He felt that such
an unflattering, ugly, weird
portrait was a betrayal, and laughter
was the only answer. Soon after
his birthday the picture disappeared.

About then, they say, Aneurin
asked Winston, 'What you got there, then?'
With an imprudent finger boring.
'If it's a girl I'll call it Elizabeth,
if it's a boy Philip. But if, as I guess
it is merely wind, I'll call it Aneurin.'

Everything came off the ration.
The women who were fond of fashion
could buy smart clothes happily
without coupons. No more
power cuts. Travel as before.
We felt we'd been set free.

In '55 Winston was sure
it was time to go. The night before
they gave a party and he caused euphoria

by his triumphant boast
to the Queen he'd often drunk this toast
to her great, great Grandmother, Victoria.

Then there was nothing and 'the black dog'
came back and lay like a vast log
in Winston's lap. Clementine was ill, and soon
there was an election. He was bereft
without a job. Clemmie wrote 'Nothing left
remarkable beneath the visiting moon'.

Winston grew very deaf and found
hearing aids buzzed with a horrid sound.
In France, in '58, he was ill, and worse,
had a relapse. Pneumonia.
The antibiotics worked but he was far
from well and needed a full time nurse.

Later that year he celebrated
his golden wedding and was feted
by Beaverbrook where they were staying
In France. A border of golden roses
was planted at Chartwell which still closes
the lawn, with all its sweetness straying.

Anthony Eden in '59
was so ill he had to resign.
The Queen sent for Winston to ask
his advice about a successor.
He went gladly and helped for
he found it a most congenial task.

He painted and traveled and played bezique
but it was a long way down from the peak,
the desperate beautiful peak of power.
People who saw him said, 'He's so clever,
tells such stories. Really, he's as good as ever.
Wonderful company, but only for half an hour'.

In the summer of '62
he broke his hip and could not do
so much afterwards. He mended
slowly, walked in a stiff manner
and said to his daughter, Diana,
'My life is over, yet it hasn't ended'.

Next year Diana took an overdose,
which was hard on Sarah who was close.
Diana had divorced Sandys and in a sense
was rudderless and depressed. Nothing new.
Mary wrote that Winston withdrew
'into a great distant silence'.

Winston and Clementine wrote.
When apart , short and loving notes.
Winston said 'In love and gaiety,
tomorrow, I understand
we will walk in the park hand in hand.
Here I have found it quite lovely'.

In '63 Winston achieved the feat
of resigning his beloved seat.
He could not fight elections. It was starred,
but after fifty years and more

in Parliament to close the door
and walk away was very hard.

A House of Commons delegation
presented Winston with a resolution.
Seven of them came to Hyde Park Gate -
Sir Alec, the opposition leaders,
the Leader and the two Elders -
and gave it to Winston with due state.

It said 'That this House desires
to put on record, as he retires,
its unbounded admiration
for his lead when Briton stood alone,
his guidance till victory was won,
and his services to the House and the Nation.'

They showed on the BBC
'A Tribute to Winston, Ninety
Years on.'. Terence Rattigan
and Noel Coward arranged it. Music hall
songs from the Boer war, the last war and all.
It gave great pleasure to the old man.

On the 11th of January
in 1965 he
had another stroke. His son-in-law,
Soames, offered the champagne he adored.
He only said, 'I'm so bored
with it all.' He'd never been before.

Mary met that ubiquitous man,

Winston's doctor, Lord Moran,
and asked him, 'Is this it?'
He answered, 'I'm afraid so.'
Seemed very gloomy and quiet and slow,
but stayed around and sighed a bit.

It soon began to be alleged
that he was ill and they were besieged:
reporters, cameramen,
though in those days all of whom
let the family go through
unquestioned. There was a bulletin.

On the 11th of January
Minnie had a son. She
was 'Little Winston's' new wife.
Randolph wrote a short note
as his mother was resting. He wrote
'In the midst of death we are in life.'

Clementine said they needed
a priest. Her daughter, Mary, heeded
her plea and phoned Philip Haylor
who dropped in and said some prayers.
in Winston's room. Clemmie shared
the worship. Winston had gone too far.

The grandchildren were scared
and rigid till they shared
the quiet room. Clemmie in her seat
holding his hand. The children could pat
the much loved marmalade cat

curled up beside his feet.

On the morning, rather early,
of the 24th of January,
most of the family began to appear.
Clementine sat by the bed
holding his hand. At the head
Randolph stood. Sarah and Mary knelt there.

The Nurses, too, were on their knees.
Winston gave two or three
long, long sighs. No one
moved or spoke. Clementine
presently asked Lord Moran
very quietly ,'Has he gone?'

The doctor nodded. One by one
they left the room to the early sun.
Later Clementine and Mary
came back. The room was filled
with a majestic presence, distilled
clearly from peace and finality.

The Queen, at an earlier date,
had said Winston was to lie in state
and have a state funeral.
This had not ever been done
since it was done for Wellington.
Two men who brought us through peril.

We were about to get married.
I was optimistic but Mark in dread

the funeral would ruin or delay
our wedding. Shaun Leslie,
Winston's cousin, came in suddenly
saying, 'You're all right, it's Saturday.'

On the 26th of January
they moved Winston's body
to Westminster Hall. At last
he lay there, guarded, and
slowly three hundred thousand
people walked silently past.

The queue was a mile long. It took
four hours to reach the Hall and look
on the coffin. The only light
seemed to come from candles and spread
from the great cross at his head.
All the rest was shadowy night.

As the endless people poured in,
soldiers stood with naked swords
at the corners of the bier.
Every twenty minutes a new starter;
on his coffin shone the Garter.
Where he'd spoken was very near.

On the 30th of January
a gun carriage took his body
to St. Paul's through the crowds.
Three thousand people were there,
including the Queen, but it seemed bare.
Most of us felt very proud.

For a long time he'd said
he'd be buried at Chartwell. Instead,
after a visit to Blenheim one day,
he decided he'd be buried
at Bladon, nearby. So he was ferried
by train to where his parents lay.

The press was asked not to come.
His family and friends were numb,
as they stood beside the grave,
with its rose wreath from Clementine
and spring-flowers wreath from the Queen.
So far had come the sinking wave.

Later that year all the family,
more than forty, went to the Abbey
to watch the Queen, all sombre and still,
unveil the stone very near
the unknown warrior. Deep and clear
it reads: 'Remember Winston Churchill.'